The World
IN THE TIME OF
ABRAHAM LINCOLN

Belitha Press

FIONA MACDONALD

First published in the UK in 1997 by

 Belitha Press Limited,
London House, Great Eastern Wharf,
Parkgate Road, London SW11 4NQ

Copyright in this format © Belitha Press Limited 1997
Text by Fiona Macdonald
Map by Robin Carter, Wildlife Art Agency

ISBN 1 85561 562 2

British Library Cataloguing in Publication Data
for this book is available from the British Library.

Series Editor: Claire Edwards
Editor: Honor Head
Art Director: Helen James
Series design: Roger Miller
Design: Jamie Asher
Picture researcher: Diana Morris
Consultant: Sallie Purkis

Printed in Hong Kong
9 8 7 6 5 4 3 2 1

Picture acknowledgements:
AKG, London: 10cr, 16, 39t.
Arcaid: 31c Lucinda Lambton.
Bridgeman Art Library: front cover c British Museum; front cover r N.P.G.
Smithsonian Institution; back cover Victoria & Albert Museum, London; 1c US
Embassy, London; 1cr British Library; 4 Private Collection; 7t US Embassy,
London; 10cl Victoria & Albert Museum, London; 10b National Library of
Australia, Canberra; 17cl British Library, London; 17cr National Library of
Australia, Canberra; 18 Private Collection; 22 Victoria & Albert Museum,
London; 23c Royal Geographical Society, London; 24 Baltimore Museum of Art,
Maryland; 25t Private Collection; 29 Royal Geographical Society, London; 37c
American Museum, Bath; 38 British Museum, London; 45 National Library of
Australia, Canberra.
British Library, India Office Collection: 27.
Trustees of the British Museum: 16b.
Corbis-Bettmann: cover drop-in, 5b, 11c, 35t, 36, 44b.
E.T. Archive: front cover l Oriental Art Museum, Genoa; 10t, 13b Musée
Malmaison; 15c; 19t National Museum of History, Lima; 21b Historical
Museum, Moscow; 28t Oriental Art Museum, Genoa; 32 Greater London

Picture acknowledgements cont:
Record Office; 43 Victoria & Albert Museum, London; 44t Bibliothèque
Nationale, Paris.
Mary Evans Picture Library: 7b, 20b, 26b, 33t, 34, 35c, 37b, 42t.
Hulton Getty Collection: 25b, 42b.
Frank Lane Picture Agency: 33b.
Mansell Collection: 21t, 23bl.
Peter Newark's Pictures: 1cl, 5t, 6b, 11t, 12, 14b, 20t, 26t, 28b, 30, 31b, 41.
North Wind Picture Archives: 11b, 13t, 15t, 19b, 39b.
Zefa: 3, 40 Damm.

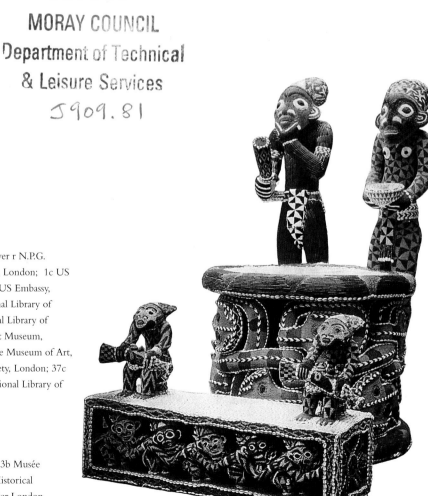

CONTENTS

ABOUT THIS BOOK

This book tells the story of Abraham Lincoln, and looks at what was happening all around the world in his time. To help you find your way through the book, each chapter has been divided into seven sections. Each section describes a different part of the world, and is headed by a colour bar. As you look through a chapter, the colour bars tell you which areas you can read about in the text below. There is a time line, to give you an outline of world events in Abraham Lincoln's time, and also a map, which shows some of the most important places mentioned in this book.

On page 46 there is a list of some of the peoples you will come across in this book. Some of the more unfamiliar words are also listed in the glossary.

THE STORY OF ABRAHAM LINCOLN

Abraham Lincoln was the sixteenth President of the United States and one of America's greatest leaders. During his lifetime many changes took place in America and around the world. In this book you can read about some of these changes. You can also read about how important Abraham Lincoln was in the history of America. Lincoln lived from 1809 to 1865 but this book covers the time period from 1800 to 1875. This will help you to discover events and ideas that influenced Abraham Lincoln and what happened in the years after he died.

◄This poster shows Lincoln at the time he became President. Above him is the White House in the city of Washington D.C., which is the official home of the President.

◄Abraham Lincoln was born in this tiny, one-roomed cabin. It had no glass in the windows and a damp earth floor.

A POOR BEGINNING

Abraham Lincoln was the second child of Thomas Lincoln, and his wife Nancy Hanks. They lived in wild countryside, known as the 'backwoods', in Kentucky, in the southeastern part of the United States. This was a harsh place to live. The weather was warm and humid in summer, but could be very cold in winter. Pioneer farmers who settled in the backwoods had to cut down thick forests and tangled shrubs before they could build their cabins to live in and plant crops.

A NEW MOTHER

Abraham's mother died when he was nine years old. The following year, Abraham's father remarried. Abraham's stepmother, Sarah Johnston, realized that Abraham was a highly intelligent, thoughtful child and she taught him to read and write. Abraham was tall and strong for his age, and his father thought this made him suitable for a life of farm work. But Sarah was convinced that Abraham had a great future ahead of him. She begged his father to give him time off from farmwork so that he could read books and study.

LEAVING THE FARM

When he was 22, Abraham left the farm and moved to the neighbouring state of Illinois where he did all kinds of jobs, including store manager, postmaster, assistant surveyor and saw-mill overseer. In 1837, after teaching himself at home, he qualified as a lawyer. Abraham became interested in politics and from 1847 to 1849 was a member of Congress. However, because he disapproved of some government policies he became unpopular and was not re-elected.

►The law offices in Springfield, Illinois, where Lincoln worked at the time he was elected President.

A DIVIDED LAND

In 1783, the United States of America won its independence from Great Britain. For a while, the new nation was united in its joy at being free. But by around 1840, the start of Lincoln's political career, there were many disagreements between different American states. The most important difference concerned slavery. In the north, slavery was illegal, but it was still legal and very popular in the south. Also, the northern states thought the President should have the power to say how all the states should be run. The southern states wanted him to have less power over them and wanted to run their own state governments by themselves.

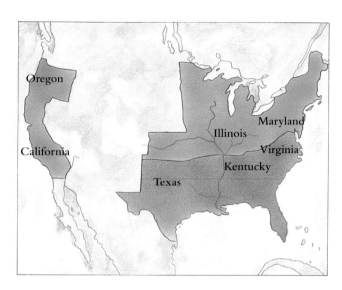

▲ The American Civil War was fought between the northern states (blue) that wanted to abolish slavery and the southern states (red) that wanted to keep slavery. The yellow area was ruled by the US government but had not yet been organized into separate states.

FIGHT AGAINST SLAVERY

Abraham Lincoln was born in a southern state, where slavery was legal, but spent all his adult life in the state of Illinois, where slavery was banned. In 1854, the US government, supported by the southern states, wanted to make slavery legal in the new frontier territories. Lincoln believed that slavery was wicked. He felt that it was very bad for the US to have states where slavery was allowed and he wanted slavery to be banned throughout the nation. In 1856 he joined the newly-formed Republican Party, and promised to fight against the spread of slavery.

◄ Sugar plantations in the southern states of America were worked by slaves. Originally, slaves were shipped to America from Africa, but by Abraham Lincoln's time many had been born to slave parents already living in America. Slaves were often cruelly treated by their owners and had no civil rights.

◄This statue of President Lincoln was made almost 100 years after he died. Today Lincoln is remembered for his fight against slavery and his belief in democracy.

CIVIL WAR

Lincoln was elected President in 1860. But soon the US was in trouble. The following year, 11 southern states broke away from the rest to form their own government. They did not want President Lincoln to ban slavery in their lands. Civil war broke out as southerners attacked northern states.

THE END OF SLAVERY

In 1862, Lincoln passed the Emancipation Proclamation, making slavery illegal everywhere in the US. He was elected President for a second term in 1864. By that time, the southern states were growing weak. Without slaves to work on their farms, landowners were becoming poor, and southern troops were short of food and weapons. But in the north, farmers, factories, shipbuilders, gun-foundries, and all the people who worked there prospered.

A NATIONAL HERO

The civil war finally ended on 9 April 1865. Thanks to Lincoln's leadership and the skills of brilliant army generals, the northern states won. Slavery was abolished throughout the US and all the states were still governed by one President. Lincoln was a hero. But Lincoln did not have much time to enjoy his achievements. On 14 April 1865, Lincoln was shot and badly wounded. He died the next day.

►Abraham Lincoln was shot while he was watching a play at a Washington theatre. His attacker was an out-of-work actor named John Wilkes Booth who supported the southern states.

THE WORLD 1800-1875

ABOUT THE MAPS

The maps on this page will help you find
your way around. The big map shows
some of the places mentioned in the
text, including:

• **COUNTRIES,** including some that are
different from modern ones.

• *Past peoples*, such as the Mandan. The
descendants of these peoples often live in
the same place today, but their traditional
lifestyles have almost vanished.

• *GEOGRAPHICAL FEATURES*, including
mountains and rivers.

• *Towns and cities.* To find the position
of a town or city, look for the name in
the list below then find the number on
the map.

1	Salt Lake City	7	Istanbul
2	Washington	8	Aden
3	New Orleans	9	Bombay
4	Charleston	10	Calcutta
5	New York	11	Canton
6	Manchester	12	Singapore

The little map shows the world divided
into seven regions. The people who lived
there were linked by customs, traditions,
beliefs, or simply by their environment.
There were many differences within each
region, but the people living there had
more in common with each other than
with people elsewhere. Each region is
shown in a different colour – the same
colours are used in the headings
throughout the book.

ARCTIC
OCEAN

RUSSIAN EMPIRE

6

CRIMEA

ALPS

7 OTTOMAN
EMPIRE

MEDITERRANEAN
SEA

SUEZ
CANAL

SAHARA
DESERT

NILE

SAUDI
ARABIA

Dinka

HIMALAYA
MOUNTAINS

CHINA   KOREA   JAPAN

INDIA

10

11

Fulani

Asanti

8

9

Masai

PACIFIC

OCEAN

EQUATOR

CONGO

ZANZIBAR

12

LAKE
TANGANYIKA

ZAMBEZI

INDIAN   OCEAN

JAVA

KALAHARI
DESERT

ST HELENA

Mthethwa
Zulus

AUSTRALIA
Aboriginals

Maoris

CAPE OF GOOD HOPE

NEW ZEALAND

KEY TO MAP

- Africa
- Americas
- Australasia
- East Asia
- Europe
- Middle East
- South Asia

TIME LINE

1800

AMERICAS

1803 US buys Louisiana (colony) from France and doubles in size.

1808–1828 Revolts by Spanish colonies in South America. 13 new countries win independence.

1808 US bans import of slaves from Africa.

1811 Shwanee leader Tecumseh leads Native American people in fighting settlers on their land. Native people defeated at the Battle of Tippecanoe.

1818 Borders agreed between US and Canada.

1812–1815 War between Britain and US.

1828 First railroad in US between Baltimore and Ohio.

EUROPE

1804 Napoleon becomes Emperor of France.

1805 Battle of Trafalgar.

1815 Battle of Waterloo.

1821 In Britain, Faraday invents the electric motor.

1825 In Britain, first passenger railway from Stockton to Darlington.

1822 In France, Niepce invents photography.

MIDDLE EAST

1804 Serbs revolt against Ottoman rule.

1811 Wahabi Saudi dynasty controls most of Arabia.

1821 Greeks revolt against Ottoman rule.

SOUTH ASIA

1815 First Gurkha regiment recruited in Nepal.
1815 British occupy Ceylon (present-day Sri Lanka).

1819 Singapore founded as a free trade port.

1825–1830 Javanese people revolt against Dutch colonial rulers.

EAST ASIA

1800 Britain begins importing opium into China.

1802 Siam (present-day Thailand) conquers Cambodia.

AFRICA

1806 British take control of Cape Colony, South Africa.

1807 Slave trade abolished throughout British Empire.

1811 Mehmet Ali takes control of Egypt.

1818 Shaka Zulu founds kingdom in South Africa.

1822 Mehmet Ali conquers Sudan.

1822 State of Liberia founded as a colony for freed slaves.

1824 Asanti people of present-day Ghana fight against British would-be colonizers.

AUSTRALASIA

1803 First circumnavigation of Australia.

1803 New British convict colony founded in Tasmania.

1810 Hawaiian Islands united.

1814 First European missionaries arrive in New Zealand.

1825 Maoris in New Zealand drive away would-be European settlers.

1875

1831 The *New York Sun*, first cheap daily paper launched.

1859 First oil well drilled in Pennsylvania.

1841 First university degrees awarded to American women.

1837 Morse Code invented by William Morse.

1860s Apache leader Geronimo (Goyanthlay) leads fight against European settlers.

1874 First electric train in New York.
1875 Telephone invented by Alexander Graham Bell.

1833 In Britain, first laws to protect factory workers.

1859 Garibaldi begins war to unite Italy.

1858 In France, Pasteur discovers that bacteria cause disease.

1861 Russian serfs freed.

1845 Famine in Ireland.

1840 First postage stamp in Britain.

1863 First underground railway in London.

1839 Britain takes control of Aden, an important trading port on the Red Sea.

1860 Revolution against Ottomans in Syria.

1869 Civil war in Lebanon.

1869 Suez Canal opens.

1853–1856 Crimean War.

1861 Bahrain becomes a British protectorate.

1853 First railways and telegraph in India.

1857 Indian Mutiny.

1843–1849 Britain conquers Sind, Punjab and Kashmir, parts of present day India and Pakistan.

1842 Britain takes control of Hong Kong.

1854 First ever treaty between Japan and USA.

1863 France takes control of Cambodia.

1839–1842 First Opium War between China and Britain.

1856–1860 Second Opium War.
1850–1864 Taiping Rebellion by Chinese against weak Chinese Emperor.

1868 Meiji dynasty comes to power in Japan and begins programme of industrialization.

1830 France begins to conquer Algeria.

1853 Livingstone begins explorations in South Africa.

1867 Diamonds discovered in South Africa.

1835 Boers begin Great Trek northwards from Cape Colony.

1840 Treaty of Waitangi – Britain takes control of New Zealand.

1851 Australian gold rush.

1860 Maori Wars between Maoris and settlers in New Zealand.

1861 Gold discovered in New Zealand.
1861 Australian women allowed to vote.

AROUND THE WORLD

During Abraham Lincoln's life, three major changes were happening around the world. Firstly, families from all over Europe left their homelands to settle in new countries, especially in America, as Lincoln's ancestors had done. Secondly, Lincoln was interested in new forms of government which would improve people's civil rights, and there were demands for similar reforms in many other countries. Thirdly, towards the end of his life, Lincoln led his country through a savage civil war. Riots and revolutions were also happening in many other lands.

▲ Fighting in the American Civil War. This painting shows northern troops capturing the southern city of St Petersberg, in April 1865.

▲ Pioneers travelling across the US faced many dangers. They had to cross wide rivers, high rocky mountains and scorching deserts.

THE US GROWS

AMERICAS

America was still a very new country when Abraham Lincoln was born. It was created in 1776 when 13 states broke away from British rule and declared themselves independent. The United States of America grew rapidly as more states joined the Union. Some were purchased, some were conquered, some were given away in peace treaties, and others, mostly to the west of the Mississippi River, were simply taken over by pioneer farmers. These new states were not empty. Native Americans had lived there for thousands of years. As settlers moved westwards, taking land from the Native Americans, there were many quarrels and fights.

NAPOLEON AT WAR

EUROPE

The early years of Abraham Lincoln's life saw dramatic events in Europe such as invasions, new governments and some of the bloodiest battles ever fought on land or sea. Much of this was caused by one person, Napoleon Bonaparte. Napoleon first won fame as a brave young soldier in the French Revolution in 1789. He lead armies throughout Europe, inspired by the ideas of 'liberty' and 'equality'. But soon he wanted power just for himself. In 1799 he seized control of the French government. In 1804 he crowned himself Emperor of France and set out to conquer as many lands as he could. At first he won many victories. He toppled many European governments and set up his own men in their place. But when he tried to invade Russia in 1812 his army ran out of food and had to retreat. Over half a million soldiers died trapped in the Russian winter snows.

► This portrait shows Napoleon giving orders to his soldiers as they march across the Alps to conquer Italy. As a ruler of France, Napoleon introduced many reforms in laws, education, and government that still influence French life today.

THE FUTURE FOR EUROPE

EUROPE

In 1815, an army from several European countries, led by Britain's Duke of Wellington, defeated the French at the Battle of Waterloo. Napoleon was forced into exile on the remote island of St Helena in the South Atlantic Ocean, where he died in 1821.

While Napeoleon was in exile an international meeting was held in Vienna, Austria to decide how Europe should be governed in future. Many kings and politicians whom Napoleon had dismissed were restored to power. But new ideas from the French revolution and from Napoleon's reforms in France had already spread to many countries in Europe, South America and the Middle East.

FREEDOM FROM SERFDOM

Over half the Russian population, about 20 million people, were serfs. This meant that they belonged to their landlord. They had to work hard for him without any pay and were not allowed to leave his lands. If they refused to obey orders they could be cruelly punished or even killed. In many ways, their lives were as terrible as the American slaves'.

Throughout the nineteenth century Russian serfs demanded freedom, but serfdom was not abolished until 1861. After Russia's defeat in the Crimean War, Alexander II became very unpopular. He feared a massive uprising if he did not agree to the serfs' demands. But even after they were freed from serfdom many Russian people were still very poor.

PEOPLE POWER

MIDDLE EAST

The Ottoman Empire was based in the city of Istanbul in Turkey. It was the most powerful state in the Middle East. But in the nineteenth century it was threatened by nationalism, the wish of conquered people to rule themselves. A revolt against the Ottomans started in Greece in 1821.

►A well-armed Greek freedom fighter. A nationalist revolt against the Ottoman Empire started in Greece. Volunteers from Britain, France and Russia helped the Greek people to fight. Greece finally won independence in 1832.

EMPIRE UNDER THREAT

The Ottoman Empire was also threatened by Russia, which had captured many Ottoman lands around the Black Sea. Russian rulers wanted access to warm-water Black Sea ports, since their own harbours were blocked by ice in winter time. Britain and France were also worried because they feared Russia would soon control all Asia, including trade routes to the rich land of India. From 1854 to 1856 Britain and France fought and won a war against Russia in the Crimea and captured the Russian port of Sevastopol.

◄The Charge of the Light Brigade took place during the Battle of Balaclava (1854) at the beginning of the Crimean War. Six hundred English soldiers on horseback and armed only with sabres misunderstood their orders. They charged towards the Russians who were armed with heavy guns. Nearly all of them were killed.

THE EAST INDIA COMPANY

SOUTH ASIA

Since the early sixteenth century, India had been ruled by emperors from the Mughal dynasty but by Abraham Lincoln's time, they were weak, and had lost control. Parts of India were ruled by Indian warrior princes, but many of the strongest, richest rulers were not Indian at all. They were a group of British merchants, working for an international trading organization called the East India Company. It had its own private army, made laws, collected taxes and controlled India's trade.

▲The city of Calcutta, in India, was founded by East India Company merchants in 1698. This view was painted in 1815.

THE INDIAN MUTINY

In 1857 Indian troops in the East India Company's army mutinied. They attacked British officers and civilians and captured many important towns. The mutiny lasted for almost a year. As a result, in 1858 the British government took control. It decided that in future India was to be ruled from London. The East India Company had its powers reduced. The last Mughal emperor was dismissed and replaced by Queen Victoria.

◄British drug dealers encouraged Chinese people to develop the dangerous habit of smoking opium by helping Chinese traders smuggle opium into China. This drawing, made around 1850, shows smugglers lowering bales of opium over a city wall.

OPIUM WARS

EAST ASIA

Chinese rulers had been so proud of their economic success and of their ancient civilization that they had refused to have any contact with the West. But Britain and other European states were keen to trade with China. They realized they could make huge sums of money through trade, especially by selling opium to the Chinese. This soon led to wars between 1836 and 1842 and 1856 and 1860. China was defeated and was forced to give European merchants the right to travel and trade throughout China.

LAND OF MANY CULTURES

AFRICA

The continent of Africa was divided into many different states. Large areas of West Africa were governed by the Fulani dynasty, who ruled their rich kingdoms according to Muslim law. West African nations, like the Asante of Ghana, had also grown rich through crafts and trade. In East Africa, the Kabakas of Buganda ruled a splendid empire in present-day Uganda and nearby lands.

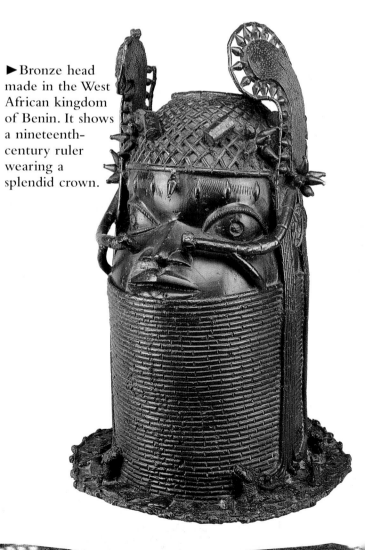

►Bronze head made in the West African kingdom of Benin. It shows a nineteenth-century ruler wearing a splendid crown.

ZULUS AND BOERS

There were troubles between British and Dutch settlers in South Africa. The British governor of the Cape tried to stop the Dutch settlers, called Boers, mistreating their African workers. But the Boers refused to obey British laws. Between 1835 and 1840, about 10,000 Boer farmers left their homes at the southern tip of Africa and trekked northwards through wild and dangerous countryside in search of new land where they could live free from British rule. Along the way, many Boers were killed by Zulu warriors when they trespassed on Zulu land.

▼ Boer farmers amd their families travelled in wagons pulled by oxen.

DISCOVERING THE SOUTH PACIFIC

AUSTRALASIA

After Captain James Cook's voyages from 1768 to 1779, European nations became aware of the vast size and richness of the South Pacific lands. They saw them as empty territory to be taken and used. They did not consider the rights of the Aboriginal and Maori people who lived there.

CONVICT SETTLEMENTS

The first Europeans to settle in Australia were the British convicts, transported there in 1788 as punishment for their crimes. Then, in 1793, the first free settlers arrived, hoping to set up ranches and farms. Eventually, released convicts also set up homes in Australia and New Zealand.

▲ Chief Palou entertaining sailors from the French ship *Astrolabe* on the Pacific island of Tonga. At first European sailors were welcomed by Pacific peoples. This friendship turned to war when European settlers started to seize their land.

WHALERS AND HUNTERS

European whalers, hunters and traders came to settle in New Zealand, and European farmers imported vast flocks of sheep to New Zealand. Between 1843 and 1872, settlers clashed with local Maori farmers in a series of fierce battles known as the Maori Wars. In a similar way, French sailors and settlers took over many Pacific Islands by force. They occupied the beautiful and very useful deep-water harbour at Tahiti in 1842.

FAMOUS RULERS AND LEADERS

In Abraham Lincoln's time rulers came from very different backgrounds and ruled in different ways. Some were born to power, like Queen Victoria, some seized it in revolutionary wars, like Simon Bolivar. Some governments were cruel and harsh, like that of Tsar Nicholas' in Russia, and some were guided by strong principles, like Lincoln's government. Many other leaders lived at this time. Some were war heroes, some worked to help other people, some put forward challenging new ideas.

◄General Ulysses S Grant (1822–1885) was leader of the victorious northern states army in the American Civil War. He won important battles against the southern states in the Mississippi Valley and Virginia. After the war, he became a politician. He was elected eighteenth President of the US in 1869.

THE GREAT ESCAPE

AMERICAS

Abraham Lincoln was only one of many people who campaigned against slavery in America. Harriet Tubman (1820–1913), an escaped slave, lived in the state of Maryland in the southern US. Together with friends, Tubman set up a network of secret trackways and overnight hiding places called 'the Underground Railroad'. It was used by slaves who had run away from their owners and were trying to reach the northern states where slavery had been banned. This was a dangerous operation. If Tubman had been caught she would have been severely punished, or even killed. When the American Civil War broke out in 1861, Tubman used her experience to undertake secret missions for Abraham Lincoln's army, as a scout and a spy.

► Historians estimate that Harriet Tubman helped about 300 slaves to escape to freedom between 1830 and 1860.

▲ Simon Bolivar, the South American revolutionary leader.

FOREIGN RULE

Ever since the sixteenth century, large parts of South America had been ruled by European nations. In the early nineteenth century, many South American colonies rebelled and declared themselves independent from European colonial rule. Simon Bolivar (1783–1830), nicknamed 'the Liberator', was the greatest South American revolutionary leader. He managed to help no less than five countries fight to win their freedom. He is still considered the 'founding father' of Venezuela, Colombia, Ecuador, Peru and Bolivia – which was named after him.

ADMIRAL NELSON

EUROPE

The top two British commanders who fought against Napoleon are still remembered as heroes in Britain. Admiral Horatio Lord Nelson (1758–1805) came from a poor clergyman's family, and joined the Navy when he was only 12 years old. After many early successes in battle, where he lost his right eye and his right arm, he was chosen to command the British fleet against the French at Trafalgar, off the coast of Spain, in 1805. He won the battle, but was wounded. He died on board his ship, the *HMS Victory*.

DUKE OF WELLINGTON

Arthur Wellesley, Duke of Wellington (1769–1852), also proved his skill when still a young man. In 1787 he was sent to India, to fight Indian princes who were rebelling against the British. He won a victory for Britain. Back in Europe, Wellington led British soldiers against Napoleon's troops when they invaded Portugal and Spain, and beat Napoleon at the battle of Waterloo in 1815. In 1820, Wellington went into politics.

▶Admiral Lord Nelson was a bold, unconventional character who was highly respected and liked by his sailors. They told many stories about his adventures, like the time he put his telescope to his blind eye to avoid seeing a signal sent by his commanding officer that he did not want to obey.

▲Victoria and Albert married in 1840 and had nine children. Prince Albert worked hard to encourage the latest developments in science and technology.

QUEEN VICTORIA

It was unusual for a woman to be head of state in Abraham Lincoln's time. Yet Princess Victoria (1819–1901) was an only child and was brought up knowing that one day she would be queen. She was given a careful education to prepare her for her future duties, and was crowned in 1837 when she was only 18 years old. She is the longest-reigning monarch in British history. Victoria married in 1840 and had nine children. Throughout her life she took a keen interest in politics and foreign affairs. Sometimes she disagreed with government policies but she tried not to interfere. At times, Victoria was not a very popular ruler. People felt she was too distant and aloof and not in touch with the lives of ordinary people. But by the end of her long reign she was loved and respected as the head of one of the richest and most powerful nations in the world.

OTTOMAN REFORMS

MIDDLE EAST

In Abraham Lincoln's time, much of the Middle East was ruled by sultans from the Ottoman dynasty, which had been in power since around 1300. Sultan Selim III (reigned 1789–1807) tried to modernize the old-style Ottoman army and government. He planned a series of changes to the tax laws and the system of land ownership. But he faced fierce opposition from traditionalists at home. Selim was forced to resign, and was then murdered by his political enemies.

▼ Tsar Nicholas I began the Crimean War by attacking the Ottoman Empire. He died before the Crimean War ended and his son took over.

▶ Ottoman sultan Abdul Majid tried to reform the ancient Ottoman Empire and stop its slow decline.

SUPERPOWERS

Later Ottoman sultans, like Abdul Majid I (ruled 1823–1861), had more success with reforms. Abdul Majid reorganized the royal court and the education system, and gave citizens better civil rights. To protect the northern part of his empire from Russian attack, he made alliances with Britain and France. Elsewhere, rulers and leaders had very different ambitions. In Afghanistan, Jamal al-Din al Afghan (1838-1897) campaigned for a union of all Islamic nations. He wanted to create a Muslim superstate. In contrast, Tsar Nicholas I of Russia (ruled 1825-1855) wanted to create a mighty Russian Empire with himself as its leader. He crushed all calls for freedom and democracy, and tried to conquer new lands by attacking Ottoman territory.

FIGHTING EUROPEAN RULE

Many of South Asia's leaders spent their lives fighting against European rule. On the rich coffee-growing island of Java, Prince Dipanegara (1785–1855) led a revolt against the Dutch colonists who had taken control of his kingdom. But his bold plans ended in tragedy. In the war that followed his revolt, between 1825 and 1830, over 200 000 Javanese people were killed, and Dipanegara was exiled.

INDIAN INDEPENDENCE

In India, Tipu Sultan, ruler of Mysore, and Laksmibai, Rani (Queen) of Jhansi, both fought bravely against the British, who wanted to take over their lands. Tipu died in the last, desperate, unsuccessful battle to save his kingdom in 1799. When British troops captured Jhansi in 1857, Laksmibai escaped, and went to join other Indian princes fighting against British rule. She was one of the bravest fighters in the battle and people at the time said she was one of the best army commanders they had ever seen. She died from wounds received in battle in 1858.

REVOLUTION IN JAPAN

EAST ASIA

In 1868, after a short civil war, a new style of government came to power in Japan. For centuries, shoguns (army generals) had run the country on behalf of the emperor. Now, new political leaders took the place of the shoguns. They were well-educated men, mostly from noble families, who had worked as government officials, but who were eager for change.

LEARNING FROM THE WORLD

Leading members of Japanese society included Kido Koin and Iwasaki Yataro. They introduced new laws, a new constitution, and new policies designed to modernize the economy and society. They encouraged foreign experts to come to Japan and went on study trips abroad. Some of these leaders, like Yataro, founded successful businesses. In 1873, he set up the Mitsubishi trading company. It dealt in banking, insurance, mining and shipping. By 1877 Mitsubishi owned 80 percent of all ships in Japan.

▼ Tipu Sultan (his name meant Tiger King) kept this lifesize model of a tiger devouring a European officer in his palace. A mechanism inside the tiger made a roaring noise.

SHAKA, KING OF THE ZULUS

In South Africa, the powerful figure of Shaka, king of the Zulu people from 1817 to 1827, played a leading part in events. The Zulus were just one small clan belonging to a much larger African nation, the Mthethwa. But Shaka wanted his people to be independent. He developed a deadly new way of fighting, using a short, stabbing spear called an assegai. Zulu warriors soon overpowered the Mthethwa nation and Shaka became king. Shaka's next plan was to win more land. The Zulus conquered vast territories in south-east Africa, forcing the African peoples who lived there to run for their lives. So many people were forced to flee that Shaka's reign became known as 'Mfecane' – 'time of troubles'.

▲ King Shaka became a hero to many Zulu people in South Africa. This drawing shows him negotiating a treaty with English army officers.

SETTLERS AND CHIEFS

In Australia and New Zealand, leaders and chiefs faced the problem of how they could stop well-armed European settlers from taking over their lands. In Australia, governors sent by Britain tried to bring peace by teaching the Aborigines European customs or by transporting them away from the settlers' land. In New Zealand quarrels between local chiefs and settlers led to fights, raids, and eventually to war.

▲ Maori warriors performing a war dance in front of a statue of a god.

TREATY OF WAITANGI

In 1840, the British government persuaded Maori chiefs to sign the Treaty of Waitangi. This said that the British would protect the Maori lands if the Maoris allowed settlers to come and live peacefully in New Zealand and let the British government rule. Thousands of British settlers flocked to New Zealand, ignored the treaty, and settled on Maori land. The British government refused to help the Maoris get their land back so, in 1843 and in 1860, the Maoris declared war. Peace was finally agreed in 1881.

HOW PEOPLE LIVED

The world in Abraham Lincoln's time was full of contrasts, especially in the way people lived. In some countries, like parts of Asia, people followed lifestyles that had changed very little in thousands of years. In other regions, like Western Europe, new inventions meant that the lives of ordinary people were changing at a dizzying pace. In Australia, Africa and parts of America, Native peoples with lifestyles that had been handed down over generations, came face to face with new settlers who had completely different customs and ideas. In most instances, the old, traditional lifestyles were destroyed by the settlers.

▲ This painting dated 1834 shows the inside of an earth lodge house. It was built by Mandan Native people who lived in present-day North Dakota.

NATIVE AMERICAN LIVES

AMERICAS

Throughout North and South America and the Caribbean, several different lifestyles existed side by side. The oldest belonged to the hundreds of Native American tribes who lived in very different environments, from high mountains to scorching deserts.

The Inuit people of the Arctic hunted seals and walrus, while along the north-west coast the Chinook trapped salmon and speared whales. On the Great Plains, the Mandan and Hidatsa hunted herds of buffalo and planted fields of maize and beans. In the western deserts, the Paiute gathered grubs, seeds and nuts. In the South American rainforests, Native peoples ate roots and fruit and hunted snakes and monkeys. Farmers in the high Andes Mountains raised herds of llamas for milk, meat and wool.

▼ A busy street in New Orleans in 1862 crowded with horse-drawn carriages and trams.

▲ Miners went to California hoping to get rich by striking gold. They dug up rocky mountain slopes or 'panned' for gold in streams.

GOLD HUNTERS

Abraham Lincoln's early life (see page 5) was typical of many farmers who moved inland from the earliest European settlements along the eastern coast. When gold was discovered in California in 1848, miners and fortune-hunters joined farmers and their families making the long, dangerous journey overland. Along the way, many died from disease and exhaustion, or after drinking poisonous water from desert springs.

CONTRASTS

In eastern cities, such as Charleston and New Orleans, there were elegant houses, hospitals, colleges, theatres, restaurants and shops. This prosperous lifestyle was, however, based on wealth created by the suffering of black slaves, who were forced to work long hours in hot, humid temperatures picking cotton and cutting sugar cane. They lived in shacks on their master's land and could be beaten or even killed if they tried to run away.

CHANGING TIMES

EUROPE

In many parts of Europe, new machines and new ways of working were transforming traditional farming and manufacturing techniques. Historians call these changes the Agricultural Revolution and the Industrial Revolution (see page 31).

THE AGRICULTURAL REVOLUTION

The Agricultural Revolution began around 1700, and continued for almost 150 years. Landowners increased farm production by introducing new crop rotations, drainage and manuring schemes, by breeding stronger cattle, and by enclosing and ploughing up commons and wasteland. These changes were profitable for landowners but caused problems for ordinary people. Many had no land of their own to grow food for their families, and without common and wasteland areas they had nowhere to graze a cow or keep a few sheep. The only regular work was on the landlords' farms, but because the population was increasing, wages were low and food prices high.

▲ In Ireland, the soil was poor and the climate was cool and wet. Ordinary people survived by growing potatoes to eat. Between 1845 and 1847, the potato crop was destroyed by blight (disease). This caused widespread famine and thousands of people died. Many of them left Ireland for a better life in the US.

◄ Life in the factory towns, which grew as a result of the Industrial Revolution, was miserable. Workers faced long hours, low pay and terrible accidents. Workers' houses were cold, cramped and dirty. Both air and water was polluted by smoke and dust from factories and there were few shops or open spaces or parks. This painting shows a typical industrial area in the Midlands, England, around 1850.

SHIPPING AND SHOPPING

MIDDLE EAST

In many parts of the Middle East, merchants and craftworkers lived in noisy, crowded towns. They sold hand-made goods, like carpets, brassware, pottery, leather saddles and slippers, in busy marketplaces called 'souks'. Ports like Aden, which were on busy shipping routes to India and beyond, grew much bigger and richer after the Suez Canal (see page 35) was opened. They sold fresh food and water to the ships, and souvenirs to the passengers on board.

CASH CROPS

In the countryside, farmers reared flocks of sheep and goats, planted apple, orange, apricot and almond orchards and olive trees, and raised crops of wheat, vegetables and melons. In Iran, they grew large fields of cash crops such as tobacco for sale to big international companies based in Europe and the US. When there was a world shortage prices were high. But if there was too much prices fell and sometimes the farmers could not afford to buy food.

CHANGES IN INDIA

SOUTH ASIA

At the beginning of the nineteenth century, many fine goods made by Indian craftworkers were exported to Europe. Brightly-coloured silks and delicate cottons were especially sought-after. The Industrial Revolution in Europe meant that machines in British factories could produce cotton cloth more cheaply than Indian hand-weavers. Now Indian farmers exported raw cotton to England and, in return, had to buy British factory-made cotton cloth. As a result, many Indian weavers were put out of work.

MANGOES AND COCONUTS

Indian farmers grew a wide variety of crops, from wheat in the north to rice, mangoes and coconuts in the south. Some of these crops went to feed farmers' families, some were paid as taxes and some were sold in market towns. Farmers' homes varied too, from sun-baked mud brick houses in the deserts of Rajasthan, to wickerwork shelters roofed with palm-leaf thatch in the hot, muddy fields of Bengal.

▶ A village in north-west India painted around 1800. Many villages were laid out according to the Hindu caste system. This divided people into four religious ranks, plus a group of 'untouchables', who were believed to be 'impure'. Top-ranking families lived in the centre of the village. Untouchables had to live outside.

GROWING POPULATION

By the early nineteenth century, the population of China had increased dramatically. For many people in the countryside life was a constant struggle to produce enough food to feed themselves and their families. In good years, when the rivers did not flood their fields, or when typhoons did not sink their fishing boats, people managed to survive. But in bad years, many starved. Others left China to work in terrible conditions building railways in Canada or digging mines and unloading ships in Malaysia and Singapore.

TREATY PORTS

During the eighteenth century, Chinese rulers kept British merchants out of China because they believed that Chinese goods were better than anything 'foreign devils' could supply. But after 1842, Chinese emperors were forced to allow European merchants to set up 'treaty ports', like the city of Canton (Guangzhou). Chinese bankers, builders, traders, craftworkers and shipowners set up thriving businesses there, and British merchants traded with immensely wealthy Chinese businessmen called taipans.

▲ A print by Japanese artist, Hiroshige, showing the traditional way of planting rice used in many East Asian lands.

TRADITIONAL LIFESTYLES

In most of Africa, traditional lifestyles continued throughout the century. On dry savannah grasslands, peoples like the Masai (of present-day Kenya) and the Dinka (of present-day Sudan) lived as herders and hunters. In tropical West Africa, people lived in farming communities and grew crops of plantains and yams. Further south, farmers grew millet and sorghum and reared cattle and goats.

◄The East African island of Zanzibar (part of present-day Tanzania) continued as a centre of slave trade long after slave trading had been abolished in West Africa.

SPLENDID TOWNS

Along the east and west coasts, there were many large and splendid towns. The West African city of Kumasi (in present-day Ghana), capital of the rich, gold-mining Asanti nation, was famous for its wide streets lined with houses decorated in shiny red and white clay. Underground drains and teams of sweepers made sure the city was kept healthy and clean.

VILLAGES AND FARMS

AUSTRALASIA

On the north island of New Zealand, Maori farmers built stone-walled villages and cleared fields. They planted crops of kumara (an orange-coloured sweet potato) and hunted moa and kiwi – huge, flightless birds. On the south island, Maori people caught fish and gathered roots and seaweed to eat. All these foods were stored in huts raised above the ground to keep them safe from dogs, rats and birds.

THE ABORIGINAL WAY

At the beginning of the nineteenth century, there were probably about 1 million Aboriginal people living in Australia. They survived in one of the harshest, driest environments in the world by using skills that had been handed down for thousands of years. These included gathering seeds and wild fruits, hunting kangaroos, fishing along the coast, trapping eels in wicker cages and birds in nets, and digging for roots and grubs.

THE NEW SETTLERS ARRIVE

In just one decade, between 1852 and 1861, over 343,000 settlers migrated to Australia from overseas. Most settlers chose to live in Australia because they hoped for a new life and a chance to get rich – either from gold-mining or from farming enormous flocks of sheep. Wool and meat from sheep were exported to Europe in large quantities to supply cloth factories and to feed the growing populations.

▶Maori village homes were built of wood. Houses like this one, which belonged to a powerful chief, were decorated with magnificent carvings of heroes and gods.

DISCOVERY AND INVENTION

During Abraham Lincoln's lifetime, there were more scientific inventions and discoveries than in any similar periods before. They took place in all areas of human knowledge from archaeology to zoology. Steam power replaced wind and water power and mass production replaced traditional craft skills. All these inventions and discoveries were made in Europe and America. They gave the countries that developed them political and economic advantages over the rest of the world.

▲ An American express train, pulled by a coal-fired locomotive, 1864. New forms of transport, such as railways and steamships, made it possible to travel much further and faster than ever before.

A CHANGING WORLD

AMERICAS

In such a vast continent as America, the development of transport and communications was especially important. In 1869 it became possible to travel right across America by train. Telegraph wires ran alongside the railway to carry urgent messages instantly. Then, in 1875, the American, Alexander Graham Bell, designed the first telephone. People could now talk to one another across thousands of miles. American inventors also invented many other things that changed people's lives, such as typewriters, sewing machines and mechanical harvesters.

FACTORY GOODS

EUROPE

In many European countries, newly-invented machines in huge factories replaced craftworkers who made goods by hand at home. Soon machines were mass-producing cloth, glass and pottery. Factories also produced cast iron, steel and cement. New materials and new building technology changed the way bridges, tunnels and tall buildings were built.

◄ A typical Industrial Revolution scene showing steel plate being made in a factory in England.

USEFUL MACHINES

Factories also produced machines like reapers and binders to help with farmwork, and steam engines to replace horses. Factories were built in towns with good supplies of water and coal to provide steam power. Millions of men, women and children moved from the country to industrial towns seeking jobs.

►The 'waterfall' lavatory, mass-produced in an English pottery factory around 1880. Thomas Crapper designed the first really efficient flush lavatory at the end of the nineteenth century.

IMPORTANT RESEARCH

Scientific researchers in nineteenth-century Europe made many important discoveries in biology, physics, chemistry, medicine and maths. Some discoveries were useful for new industries, like the invention of long-lasting fabric dyes, electricity and extra-strong kinds of steel. Some, like the discovery of antiseptics and anaesthetics, improved the quality of medical help. Some, like Babbage's 'difference engine' (computer) of 1823 and Niepce's experiments with photography (1827), paved the way for inventions that would be very important in later years.

NEW WAYS OF WAR

EUROPE

During the nineteenth century, new inventions and discoveries changed the way wars were fought. The Crimean War (see pages 14 to 15) was the first war in which breech-loading rifles were used – they were faster to load and fire than earlier types of guns. It was also the first war in which underwater mines fitted with explosives and a detonator (a device to make them go off) were used to sink enemy ships. Wartime events also encouraged scientific research. After the French Black Sea fleet was badly damaged by an unexpected storm, army and navy commanders began to demand more accurate weather forecasting and scientists in many lands began to keep more detailed records of the weather.

SHOCKING NEWS

For the first time, army commanders in the Crimean War used the newly-invented electric telegraph to send urgent messages to government leaders. Journalists also telegraphed reports to their newspapers. Readers were shocked when they read these eyewitness accounts of the terrible fighting and saw the first-ever newspaper photos of battle scenes and men injured in war.

▼ More men died during the Crimean War from dirt and disease than in battle. When British nurse, Florence Nightingale, arrived in the Crimea, she was appalled at the conditions she found there. She immediately organized proper hygiene and better nursing care. Later, she set up schools where professional nurses could be trained.

◄In areas of South Asia, such as north-east India and Sri Lanka, huge tea plantations were created by European estate-owners. Local women picked tea leaves by hand which were then dried in the sun and packed in wooden chests. The chests were loaded on to fast, sleek, sailing ships called clippers, and the tea transported to Europe.

RAW MATERIALS

SOUTH ASIA

The Industrial Revolution in Europe led to huge demands for a wide range of raw materials from Asia, especially plant fibres grown in India, such as cotton and jute. Cotton was woven and sewn in English factories to make clothing and household textiles like towels, sheets and curtains. Jute was used for floor coverings and rope. In other South Asian countries, the needs of European industry led to new crops being introduced. In 1876, the first rubber trees were planted in Malaya. Their sticky sap was collected and sent to Europe for use in waterproofing and to make rubber tyres.

HELP FROM THE WEST

EAST ASIA

During the nineteenth century, railways were an important sign of how forward-thinking a country was. In Japan, the first railway opened in 1872, four years after the Meiji government came to power. Japanese rulers employed foreign experts to advise them on on how to set up the latest communications systems, such as a postal service.

WORLD EXPLORATIONS

Russia ruled an enormous empire in Siberia and East Asia, and nineteenth-century Russian scientists were keen to investigate these wild and remote lands. The Russians were great sea-explorers, too. In 1820, Russian navigator von Bellinghausen and two of his colleagues became the first people to catch sight of the vast, frozen continent of Antarctica.

WILD FRONTIERS

MIDDLE EAST

Russia ruled many lawless regions of the Middle East, which bordered the lands of the Ottoman Empire. Because Russia and the Ottomans were often at war, Russian army commanders needed to be able to transport troops and supplies safely and quickly to areas of fighting. The newly-invented railways seemed to be the answer. In the 1870s, Russian military engineers began to plan a railway from the Middle East to Afghanistan. Locomotives were designed that would run on naphtha, a by-product of the oil refineries that were being built in large numbers in the Middle East.

THE UNKNOWN CONTINENT

AFRICA

At the beginning of Abraham Lincoln's lifetime, people in Europe and America knew very little about Africa, except for the Dutch and British settlements in South Africa and the ports around the coast. They did not understand African cultures and were mostly ignorant of the great civilizations that had existed in Africa in the past. During the nineteenth century, missionaries and scientists explored the African interior, making their way slowly and painfully through rainforests and across deserts, charting high mountains, great rivers and vast lakes. By the end of the century, the spectacular scenery and wildlife of Africa were known and admired throughout the world.

LIVINGSTONE IN AFRICA

Scottish doctor and missionary, David Livingstone (1813-1873), was one of the most famous European explorers. He set up a mission station in Botswana, crossed the Kalahari Desert, and explored the Zambezi river. He spent the last years of his life searching for the sources of the River Congo and the River Nile. For three years, Livingstone vanished without a trace. Journalist Henry Morton Stanley (1841–1904) went to Africa to try and find him. They met on the shores of Lake Tangyanika in 1871. Livingstone died two years later, worn out by travelling and malaria.

▼ David Livingstone spent many years exploring Africa. In this painting he has reached Lake Ngami in the Kalahari Desert.

DISCOVERY AND INVENTION   35

▲ A dredger at work in the Suez Canal soon after it was opened. The canal needed constant dredging. This involved scooping mud from the bottom of the canal to keep its deep-water channels open for use by ocean-going ships.

THE SUEZ CANAL

In 1859, French engineer Ferdinand de Lesseps and gangs of Egyptian workers began to build a new canal to join the Mediterranean with the Red Sea. It took them ten years to complete. It was named after Suez, the port where it joined the Red Sea, and was opened in 1869. The Suez Canal revolutionized travel and trade between Europe, India, Australia and the Far East.

CONTROLLING THE CANAL

Because of the Suez Canal, ships no longer had to make the long, dangerous voyage around the southern tip of Africa. Journey times and shipping costs were reduced. The canal also made north-east Africa very important politically. European nations wanted to control it so that they could safeguard their ships in the canal. In 1882, Britain made Egypt a 'protectorate', and, in 1898, took over the government of the Sudan.

ANCIENT SKILLS   AUSTRALASIA

The Aboriginal people of Australia developed skills which enabled them to survive in a very harsh environment. They knew how to find underground water in the desert and how to make poisonous plants safe to eat. But this knowledge was ignored by most nineteenth-century Europeans in Australia. They were confident in their own skills, like map-making and surveying, and did not think they needed help from the Aboriginals. In 1861, European explorers Burke and Wills made the first-ever crossing of Australia from south to north. They ignored the advice of the Aboriginals on how to survive the journey back and died of starvation and thirst.

▲ Exhausted members of Burke and Wills' expedition close to Mount Hopeless, Australia, 1861.

FROZEN FOODS

In New Zealand, one important scientific advance benefited European settlers far more than the native Maori people. In 1882, the first refrigerated ship reached London from New Zealand, carrying 'fresh, frozen' meat and butter. Now settlers in New Zealand could sell their farm produce to a wider European market, and make more money too.

THE CREATIVE WORLD

For thousands of years, people all around the world worked with simple tools, such as brushes, chisels, looms and potters' wheels, to create beautiful paintings, statues, fabrics and pottery. In Africa, Asia, and parts of eastern Europe, works of art continued to be produced using traditional techniques. But by Abraham Lincoln's time, the traditional ways of creating things were beginning to change in America, Western Europe, and many European countries. Men and women who enjoyed making things were now using their creative talents to design new machines, from computers to combine harvesters. And new processes were being invented, such as photography, that relied on science to help create works of art.

▲ Drum made by the Chippewa Native people, who lived in the Great Lakes region of North America. It is decorated with a painting of a magical bird. Musical instruments were used in religious ceremonies, and by shamans, to communicate with the spirit world.

A CHANGE OF STYLE

Long before the first settlers arrived in North and South America, there was a fine tradition of Native American art. Native craftworkers produced beautifully-decorated clothes, jewellery, pottery, rugs and baskets for everyday use, as well as many carvings, knives, statues, bowls and pipes. By Abraham Lincoln's day, these ancient Native American traditions were in danger of being overtaken by new artistic styles brought over from Europe by the new settlers.

◀The art and craftwork of American settlers was often very attractive. This graceful chair was made by members of the Shaker community.

ART FOR ALL

During the nineteenth century, new inventions changed the way art was created in many parts of Europe. Manufacturing processes developed for heavy industry were used to create art. Pottery, furniture, carpets and even musical instruments were mass-produced in factories. For the first time, machines could produce cheap copies of an artist's work. Novels by popular writers like Charles Dickens were often published in weekly instalments in magazines. Better-off people could afford to buy sheet music with tunes by leading composers, like Liszt and Beethoven.

NEW TECHNIQUES

Improved technology also created the possibility of new forms of architecture, which relied on new materials and new building techniques. Wallpapers and curtain fabrics were also available printed with designs using new chemical dyes.

▶The Crystal Palace in London, England was a huge hall built of the new, factory-made materials, glass and cast iron. It was built to hold the Great Exhibition of 1851, which was a display of all the latest industrial machinery and mass-produced goods being made in British factories.

MAGIC CARPETS

MIDDLE EAST

Carpets were an ancient Middle Eastern art form, ideally suited to nomad life. Unlike heavy, bulky, fragile furniture, they could be packed up and transported with speed and ease. Beautiful carpets, made of silk or wool or a combination of both, were produced in many Middle Eastern lands throughout the nineteenth century. Other traditional arts, especially metalwork and calligraphy (fine writing), also thrived.

►These shadow puppets are from Indonesia. The big puppet is of a wise holy man and the small puppet is a servant girl. They are made of painted leather on a wooden frame. Shadow puppets are still a popular form of storytelling in South Asia.

CLOTH AND PUPPETS

SOUTH ASIA

All kinds of beautiful batik cloths were created in Indonesia and nearby lands. Batik cloths were plain pieces of material that were dyed in glowing colours to create complicated and fascinating patterns. In the same countries, graceful shadow puppets were used to entertain audiences with plays based on folk-tales and religious stories hundreds of years old.

WOOD BLOCK PRINTS

EAST ASIA

In Japan, wood block prints, made for sale to wealthy, well-educated collectors, were the most popular art form in the eighteenth and nineteenth centuries. The work of two great master printers, Hokusai and Hiroshige, is still admired and reprinted even today. Hokusai specialized in landscapes, such as those showing holy places like Mount Fuji, or dramatic sea scenes. Hiroshige's prints are softer and gentler, and use flowers, clouds and trees to create a tranquil, melancholy mood. (You can see one of Hiroshige's wood block prints on page 28).

INDIAN CRAFTS

Traditional arts and crafts were created in India too, such as paintings, jewellery, carvings and statues. But many Indian craftworkers were also employed to produce goods especially for export to Europe, including silk and cotton fabrics patterned with European-style versions of ancient Indian designs. Indian workers constructed many fine buildings, such as the Bombay Railway Station, in an elaborate mixture of Indian and European styles.

UNCHANGED TRADITIONS

In many parts of Africa, arts and crafts continued to be made using traditional methods. In West Africa, craftsmen carved wonderful statues and masks out of wood, hammered and twisted pure gold into large pieces of jewellery, and made heads and magic animal statues out of brass and bronze. Weavers and dyers created beautiful, brightly-patterned textiles – some of the finest were worn only by kings and queens.

FULANI MOSQUES

Builders working for the Fulani dynasty of rulers in West Africa designed remarkable dome-shaped mosques, covered all over with a thick thatch of grass. These roofs were based on traditional house roofs and kept heavy tropical rainfall off the worshippers inside.

►Only a chief could sit here! This magnificent wooden throne was carved by craftworkers in the African kingdom of Cameroun.

▲This is a tattooed hunter from the Marquesas Islands in the Pacific, 1813. Many Pacific people believed that the gods themselves were tattooed.

THE ART OF TATTOOING

In New Zealand and the Pacific Islands wood carvers made statues of gods and nature-spirits, and decorated houses and canoes with elaborate wooden carvings in traditional swirling designs. Similar patterns were used to decorate people's bodies. Tattoos were worn by many Maori warriors as a sign of courage and pride. Stories from New Zealand explain that tattooing in a special spiral pattern was brought to earth by the legendary hero Mata-Ora after he had visited the gods.

BELIEFS AND IDEAS

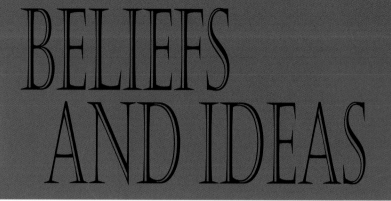

In many parts of the world, the nineteenth century was a time of rapid change. New scientific discoveries made people think again about their religious and political beliefs, and there were urgent calls for progress and reform. Sometimes, as in European countries, new ideas came from within. In other countries, such as Japan, new ideas were the result of contacts with people from elsewhere. Old and new beliefs existed side by side. But in places like America, where non-Native ideas threatened to completely wipe out traditional Native beliefs, these clashes led to war.

◄This totem pole is from the Pacific coast of Canada. Totem poles were made to honour the memory of family ancestors. They also represented guardian spirits in the shape of animals and birds.

MOTHER EARTH

AMERICAS

Each Native American tribe had its own religious customs and ceremonies, and its own myths and legends. But all tribes respected the natural world and believed that the earth was their 'Mother'. They also believed that all living things – animals, rocks, rivers – had their own invisible spirits with the power to help or harm. Offerings of all kinds, such as gifts of food and drink and displays of dancing, were made to please these spirits.

MISSIONARIES

The earliest European settlers in America were mostly Christians. They built churches and schools and sent missionaries to North and South America to try and convert Native Americans. These missionaries did not always succeed. For example, in South America and the Caribbean, their Christian teaching became mixed with traditional beliefs to create a new faith.

BLESSED BY GOD

Many European settlers believed that Native American civilization was primitive. They thought that European religious beliefs were superior and had been blessed by God. They believed that the European lifestyle was destined to replace Native American ways.

NEW RELIGIONS

During Abraham Lincoln's time, many new religious ideas grew in America. In 1847 a preacher called Joseph Smith believed he had been sent special messages from God. He led his people overland to the Wild West. Here they set up a new community in Salt Lake City, Utah, based on the teachings of Smith's new Mormon religion.

In 1774 a group of Shakers settled in New York State. Their community grew during the nineteenth century. The Shakers lived simply, making their own furniture and growing their own food. They did not believe in marriage and refused to go to war.

►The Shakers originated in England. They migrated to America looking for religious freedom. Their religious worship included trembling, dancing and falling into trances.

THE RIGHT TO BE FREE

EUROPE

Slavery was a controversial issue in Europe, as well as in the US. Anti-slavery activists, led by British MP William Wilberforce, campaigned for 20 years before the slave trade was banned by Britain in 1807. Slavery itself was not made illegal in Britain until 1833. Wilberforce was supported during his campaign by his deeply-held Christian beliefs. He and his followers were nicknamed 'the Saints'. France and Spain followed Britain's example, and banned their own ships from slave trading in 1818 and 1820.

▼ This nineteenth-century picture of an African slave was done to celebrate Wilberforce's success in getting the slave trade banned. The slave in the picture is about to be freed.

▲ Eleven peaceful protesters were killed by soldiers in the Peterloo Massacre which took place in St Peter's Fields, Manchester, England.

THE RIGHT TO VOTE

In England, protesters demanded that Parliament should be reformed so it could better represent the views and needs of ordinary people. They also wanted working men to be given the right to vote. These demands increased after an incident in Manchester in 1819, known as the Peterloo Massacre. Soldiers fired into a crowd of peaceful protesters who were demanding parliamentary reform. Eleven people were killed. Eventually, in 1832 and 1867, Parliament passed laws to increase the number of people who were allowed to vote. But this right was not given to all adult men until 1918. Women had to wait until 1928 before they could vote on the same terms as men.

REVOLUTIONARY IDEAS

In mainland Europe there were also demands for government reform. In 1848, the Year of Revolutions, there were riots in many European cities. In the same year, Karl Marx, a German writer living in London, published a book called the *Communist Manifesto*. In it he demanded greater freedom and better pay for ordinary people. He urged: 'Workers of the world unite! You have nothing to lose but your chains!'

HUMAN ORIGINS

New scientific ideas excited many people in nineteenth-century Europe. They were fascinated by the discoveries made by naturalist Charles Darwin on his expedition to study wildlife in South America between 1831 and 1836. A few years later, they were shocked when Darwin published his ideas on how man evolved. He argued that human beings were descended from apes, not created from dust as the Bible says.

REFORMS

MIDDLE EAST

Over the centuries, Muslim communities in the Middle East had developed different ways of worshipping Allah (God). These included singing, dancing and visiting the tombs of saints and Sufis. But by Lincoln's time, a group of religious reformers called Wahabis (named after their founder Muhammad ibn Abd-al-Wahab) believed these were wrong. They wanted simpler ways of worship and a return to laws based on the Muslim holy book, the Qur'an. Wahabi ideas inspired Sheik Muhammad ibn Saud to unite almost all the lands of Arabia into a single kingdom, ruled by Muslim laws.

THE DIVINE SOCIETY

SOUTH ASIA

In India, religious beliefs and political ideas were mingled together. Most Indian people followed the Hindu faith, although there were many Buddhists, Muslims, Sikhs and Parsees. In 1828 a Hindu religious reformer, Rajah Ram Mohan Roy, founded the Divine Society. This was a religious movement which aimed to ban ancient rituals from Hindu religious ceremonies. For example, he banned idol worship and suttee – the custom which forced a wife to commit suicide when her husband died. He also campaigned for Indians to have the right to govern their own land.

► Kali was the Indian goddess of bloodshed and death. Her followers believed that it was their duty to murder people as offerings to her.

INVISIBLE SPIRITS

Most people in East Asia followed three ancient, traditional religions – Confucianism, Taoism and Buddhism. But some people, especially in Mongolia, Korea and Japan, also worshipped invisible spirits. They believed these spirits lived in mountains, rivers and trees. Special priests called shamans believed they could enter the spirit world by ritual chanting, drumming and dancing and sometimes by taking drugs. Shamans worked to help the community. They tried to find good hunting grounds, control the weather, drive away bad luck and heal the sick.

◄This shaman from north-east Asia is dressed in magnificent robes decorated with amulets and charms. He is carrying a drum to call up the spirits and a stick with little jingling bells.

GODS, KINGS AND PRIESTS

AFRICA

In Africa, religious ideas varied from nation to nation. But most African people believed in a god (or several gods) who protected their homeland, gave them children, made the rains fall and helped their crops and livestock to grow. Sometimes the gods spoke through kings or priests, sometimes they were represented by carved statues or masks. African people also believed in powerful spirits which could bring good luck, or disease and disaster. They believed that the spirits of dead ancestors could help them if they were treated with respect. So families made offerings to ancestor spirits at special shrines, where the bones of dead ancestors were kept in beautifully-decorated containers carved from wood.

◄Masks were worn in many different African religious ceremonies. They might represent dead ancestors or holy spirits. Some masks were believed to have special powers of their own.

MISSIONARIES

After around 1860, many Christian missionaries from Europe arrived in Africa and began to teach their own faith. They felt it was their duty to 'save the souls' of people who had never heard of Jesus. Many missionaries gave their lives to this cause. Some died from tropical diseases and some were murdered by African leaders who feared the missionaries' teaching would destroy their people's ancient way of life.

HOLY PEOPLE

AUSTRALASIA

In Australia and New Zealand gods, spirits and dead people, such as family ancestors, were honoured in special ceremonies with singing and dancing. Sometimes, people going through personal ceremonies, such as one to mark the change from childhood to adulthood, were treated as if they were holy. In New Zealand, being tattooed was a sign of reaching adulthood. During a tattooing ceremony, food was not allowed to touch the tattooed person's lips, so it was poured down their throat using a special wooden funnel.

GHOSTS AND DEMONS

The peoples of the Pacific Islands worshipped many different gods. Each god or goddess had their own special powers – creating dry land, controlling animals and plants, sending good harvests, causing earthquakes, or bringing rain. These gods and goddesses might appear in all kinds of terrifying shapes and forms, such as erupting volcanoes, sea-monsters or ghosts. Pacific Islanders also feared the spirits of dead people, which haunted burial grounds. They thought that some spirits were seeking a final resting place beyond the sea and the sky. They thought others were looking for new spirit bodies, which they would enter and take over and be reborn as dangerous demons.

▼ Aboriginal dancers taking part in a religious ceremony called a corrobboree in Tasmania in 1830. They painted their bodies to look like spirits from the Dreamtime, a magical age long ago when ancestors and spirits created the world. The ceremony takes place at night.

PEOPLES FROM AROUND THE WORLD

GLOSSARY

Aboriginals The first inhabitants of Australia who arrived there about 40,000 years ago.

Asanti The people who lived in present-day Ghana, Togo and the Ivory Coast. Also the name of an independent kingdom in the same region of Africa during the 1700s and 1800s.

Chinook People who lived on the north-west coast of America. They caught fish and carved huge totem poles.

Chippewa People who lived in the Great Lakes region of North America. They were hunters and farmers.

Dinka Semi-nomadic cattle-herding people who lived in the Upper Nile valley, part of present-day Sudan.

Fulani A group of Muslim cattle-herding peoples from Africa who set up a powerful kingdom in the early 1800s.

Hidatsa People who lived in the Missouri River valley in present-day North Dakota, US. They built earth lodges, farmed maize and hunted buffalo.

Inuit Native Americans who arrived in the Arctic regions of North America about 2000 BC.

Mandan People who lived in the Missouri River valley, in present-day North Dakota, US. They built earth lodges, farmed maize and hunted buffalo.

Maori Settlers in New Zealand who came from the Pacific islands from about 800 AD.

Masai Hunters and cattle-herders who lived on the savannahs (dry grasslands) of East Africa in present-day Kenya and nearby.

Mthethwa The people who controlled southern Africa before the Zulus became powerful.

Native Americans The first inhabitants of America, who arrived there about 30,000 years ago. Native American people were divided into more than 200 different nations, with different lifestyles and languages.

Native Peoples The original inhabitants of any country or the people who have been born and brought up there.

Paiute Nomad people who lived in the dry Great Basin region of North America. They survived by gathering wild foods.

Zulus A group of peoples who lived in southern Africa. In the early 1800s, led by Shaka, they joined together and conquered a large empire. Zulu power collapsed in 1879 after Zulu warriors were defeated by European settlers.

amulets Lucky charms.

archaeology The study of the past from remains such as bones, coins, pottery and the ruins of old buildings.

assassinated Killed by political enemies.

batik A type of cloth, produced in Indonesia and nearby lands. It is decorated by painting patterns on the cloth with wax, then dying it using brilliant colours. The area painted with wax does not absorb the dye. The wax is removed from the cloth, leaving elaborate designs made up of dyed and undyed areas of fabric.

blight A disease (usually of plants) that causes them to wither and rot.

Buddhism A religion based on the teachings of prince Gautama Siddhartha who lived in India in the sixth century BC. He taught his followers to seek truth and the right way to live through meditation (quiet thinking).

Christian A person who believes in and follows the teachings of Jesus Christ.

civil rights Giving ordinary people the right to play a full part in society by allowing them to vote, receive an education, have a job, marry and have children, and follow their own religious faith.

civil war A war between different groups of people within one country.

colonial Belonging to a colony – a country or region that is is ruled by a stronger, foreign power.

commons Open spaces of countryside where villagers had rights to feed animals and gather firewood.

Confucianism A way of living based on the teachings of Confucius who lived in China 551-479 BC. He believed in the good of old customs and traditions.

Congress Part of the government of the US. Members of Congress debate government policies, vote to collect taxes, and make new laws.

democratic Used to describe a system of government where ordinary people have a right to choose their leaders and to comment freely on government policies.

drainage Digging ditches and installing underground pipes so that surplus water can flow away.

emancipation Often used to mean 'freedom from slavery'.

French Revolution The period 1789-1794 when the people of France rebelled against the French king and queen and executed them along with thousands of nobles and priests. They then introduced a new form of government based on the principles of 'Liberty' (freedom) and 'Equality'. The Revolution collapsed after revolutionary leaders argued among themselves and because many French people became sickened by the fighting and bloodshed.

frontier A boundary between different nations.

government policies What a government plans and does.

gun foundries Specialist factories and workshops where metal guns were made.

HMS His (or Her) Majesty's Ship - part of the the name given to all warships in the British Navy.

humid Hot and moist.

improved cattle Cattle that grew bigger and stronger and produced more meat.

maize Sweetcorn.

manuring schemes The scientific spreading of manure (animal dung) on the farmland to improve it. Manure added important chemicals to the soil and made crops grow better.

mosques Buildings where Muslims gather to say prayers and listen to readings from the Muslim holy book, the Qur'an.

naturalist Someone who studies wild animals and plants.

Ottoman Empire The lands ruled by members of the Ottoman dynasty (ruling family) in eastern Europe, North Africa and the Middle East. The Ottoman capital city was in Istanbul, Turkey.

paddy fields Flooded fields where rice is grown.

panning for gold Searching for gold by sieving the fine silt at the bottom of rivers in the hope of finding tiny fragments of gold.

people A group which lives together as one nation, or which is united under one government or by religious faith or origins.

plantains Fruit related to bananas, usually picked while green and cooked before eating.

proclamation Official announcement.

protectorate A country that has been taken over by a stronger country which offers to protect it.

Republican Party A political party in the US, founded in 1854 to fight against slavery.

sabres Long, curved swords.

savannah Dry, rolling grasslands.

saw-mill A factory where tree-trunks are sawn into planks of wood.

sorghum A grass-like plant that produces edible seeds, which can be ground to make flour or boiled to make porridge.

state governments The elected rulers who governed all the separate states in the US.

Sufis Muslim mystics – people who devoted their lives to prayer and meditation (quiet thinking) about God.

surveyor Someone whose job it is to measure and value land and buildings.

Taoism A way of living based on the belief that returning to nature is the right way to live.

tribe Closely-knit social group, usually made up of related families who follow one leader.

typhoons Violent tropical storm, from the Chinese words for 'big wind'.

yam Tropical plant which produces edible roots.

zoology The study of animals.

INDEX